MY YEAR LIVING WITH FRED AND ROSE WEST IN THE HOUSE OF HORRORS

NIGHTMARE ON CROMWELL STREET

KAREN HAMILTON

HEMBURY
—BOOKS—

About the Author

Karen Hamilton was born in Sydney's eastern suburbs and spent her childhood in the blue waters of the Pacific Ocean. Throughout her early life she travelled extensively with her family and grew connected to the small English town of Gloucester where her aunt and uncle resided. When she returned to Australia in the late 1970s, Karen began her career working as a secretary for the Department of Foreign Affairs in Canberra.

Karen later became an audio typist for police interviews, a position she has held for 25 years. She has also worked as a court reporter across Australia. It was her professional ties to the criminal justice system, coupled with harrowing personal experiences, that drew her towards true crime as a genre.

In her spare time, Karen contributes to Australian magazines like New Idea, where she writes opinion pieces on pop culture, true crime and breaking news. Karen now lives in the western suburbs of Sydney, nestled underneath the majestic Blue Mountains.

HEMBURY
—BOOKS—

Copyright © Karen Hamilton 2026
First published by Hembury Books in 2026
hemburybooks.com.au
info@hemburybooks.com

Hardback ISBN 9781923517752
Ebook ISBN 9781923517547

The moral right of the author has been asserted.
All rights reserved. No portion of this book may be reproduced in any form without permission from the author and publisher, except as permitted by Australian copyright law.

NATIONAL
LIBRARY
OF AUSTRALIA

A catalogue record for this book is available from the National Library of Australia

To Shirley Robinson and other the innocent young women who lost their lives in Cromwell Street.

A huge thank you to my friends and family who were supportive and positive throughout the writing of this dark part of history.

With a special thanks to my son, Dane, for his amazing artistry.

To my long-lost friend Liz, whom I will miss forever.

CONTENTS

Prologue 8

Chapter One – The Very Beginning 10

Chapter Two – Return to Sydney 13

Chapter Three – Gloucester in 1970 16

Chapter Four – My New Friend Liz 23

Chapter Five – Meeting Fred and Rose: Stepping into the Web 26

Chapter Six – The Bedsit 38

Chapter Seven – Gossip 51

Chapter Eight – The Return to Gloucester 55

Chapter Nine – Meeting Shirley Robinson 59

Chapter Ten – Back to Sydney Again 63

Chapter Eleven – 1994 – Shock News – 'The House of Horrors' 66

Chapter Twelve – The End of the Nightmares 74

Acknowledgements 77

Prologue

This book is my recollection of events that occurred almost fifty years ago, when I was living in the 'House of Horrors' on 25 Cromwell Street, Gloucester, England. It was the home of serial killers Fred and Rose West, who murdered their own daughter as well as several of their lodgers and buried them under the patio in their backyard and in their cellar. I was a friend of one of their lodgers and lived there for almost a year while I was on a Working Holiday visa in the UK. This story is about how I somehow slipped through the grasp of two of the most infamous serious killers in English history.

It is a book about supernatural experiences, eerie occurrences and signs that something was not quite right. The murders Fred and Rose West committed were hidden from the public until eighteen years after my stay in that house. Fred and Rose West's diabolical behaviour went on for years, until it was discovered in 1994. Their house held secrets of young women who went missing, later to be discovered buried beneath their home. At the time the crimes were exposed, some of the bodies had been decaying there for more than twenty years.

The victims were all naive young women, often runaways and children in care, who were murdered in the prime of their lives. They trusted a seemingly innocent couple, who dragged them down to their cellar to torture and kill them before a hidden burial under concrete slabs or in the cellar. It is difficult to imagine such cruelty and how the victims must have felt. The fact that they murdered their own daughter beggars belief.

It is also a story of friendships made and lost. Although many years have passed since my year spent at this infamous house, the memories have never left me. They have plagued me throughout my life. I hope that by recollecting them, I will find a greater sense of peace.

The memories in this book date back over 50 years, so of course I don't recall every detail. Rather than embellish my story or pad it out, I have only included what I am confident I can accurately recall. As a result this memoir is not long, as I have told my story as truthfully as I can.

Chapter One

THE VERY BEGINNING

My parents emigrated from England to Australia and settled in the Eastern Suburbs of Sydney some years after World War II. My father had been a highly decorated pilot in the Royal Air Force during the war. When he crashed his plane in Burma, he and some of his troop escaped into the jungle. My dad was rescued by people from the Karen ethnic group, and I was later named Karen in their honour. These wonderfully kind Burmese villagers passed my father from village to village on a stretcher, keeping him safe from the surrounding enemy and saving his life.

In 1947 he became the personal pilot for Aung San, a revolutionary and a former Prime Minister of Burma who negotiated Burma's independence from British colonial rulers. They became close friends until Aung San's assassination. My father was waiting on the tarmac at the time and was told to fly away because Aung San had been murdered. His daughter, the future democratic leader Aung San Suu Kyi, was only four years old at the time. My father spoke fondly of his beloved friend

Chapter One – THE VERY BEGINNING

over the decades—he even had an old photograph of himself and Aung San both in uniform on display until his death at the age of ninety-one.

Some years after the war ended, my parents decided to move to Australia. The warm tropical climate and cool winters would have been intoxicating after the UK's bleak weather. My father had four brothers and two sisters and they nearly all made the journey to Australia to start a new life, as did many Europeans back then, although one brother decided America was his destination. They settled primarily in the Eastern Suburbs of Sydney, close to the beaches, and along with other relatives, enjoyed a quiet family life.

After a ten-year period of settling down and living in Australia, and now with a little family of their own, homesickness eventually crept in. My parents packed up and flew to England with me and my brother to catch up with relatives. It would be a whirlwind of parties and get-togethers. I remember meeting the odd family member I didn't know existed and it all seemed a mass of happy faces. I met cousins that I had never met before and it truly was very exciting. All the family on both sides lived in Gloucester, so it was easy for us to get together. We took in all the beautiful places in England, the hamlets and gorgeous scenic routes that one does when visiting this exquisite country that is steeped in so much history and grandeur. The vivid greenery and rich foliage surrounding Gloucester is still etched into my memory.

This first visit to was only for a month, so it was jam-packed with things to take in and fall in love with. I remember that all the children played outside until around ten p.m. as it didn't get dark until then. Back in Sydney the sun went down much earlier. I had to be in bed by eight, and I could still hear my new friends running up and down the street, laughing and screaming in glee, shouting for us to come back outside. I thought it was very strange that it was not yet dark by the time I went to bed. It felt unfair that I was missing out on the fun.

We stayed in my uncle and aunt's terrace, which was at 15 Cromwell Street—five doors down from Fred and Rose West's home. Back then it was a very quiet street lined with narrow terrace houses. I found them unusual as I only knew bungalows back home—all these houses were kind of stuck together. 15 Cromwell Street in the middle of Gloucester was a regular-looking terrace house. It had three floors and a heavy front door. My bedroom was at the top of the narrow staircase, and overlooked a long, thin backyard covered in lush green foliage. It was like having my own English countryside outside my bedroom. I never grew tired of peering out the window, as the air would always be so fresh and sweet.

The rooms were small compared to what I was used to back home, but they were cosy and full of brightly coloured ornaments. There seemed to be so many rooms as I walked up the stairs. Instead of them being spread out like they were in the houses I knew in Australia, the rooms in 15 Cromwell Street were all connected to the stairs, so on the way up to the top floor, the bedroom doors would be to your right or left. My three male cousins lived there too, and we would hang out in the backyard if it was not too cold or wet.

We didn't spend a lot of time in the terrace as we travelled around, even venturing to Scotland to visit Dad's war buddies. We would always return to Cromwell Street before venturing somewhere different the next day. Even back then, at the tender age of ten, the street gave me a sense of quiet while still softly bustling with neighbours and people walking past. The community within the street showed a lot of kindness towards each other. I would play with the children in the street, and we would venture out for as long as we were allowed. The houses all had different-coloured front doors, and this was how I knew where my friends lived. Everything seemed very neat and orderly.

Chapter Two

RETURN TO SYDNEY

After our glorious four weeks visiting various places and family, it was time to say goodbye to everyone and fly back to Australia. It would have been heart-wrenching for my parents to say goodbye, but we at least flew back home with amazing memories. I think of my parents having an invisible elastic band wrapped around them, stretching and pulling them tightly between two places, loving them both.

We returned home to continue with our lives on the other side of the world. After a year or so, my parents decided to go back to England and buy a business; start another new life in England. This time they decided to travel by sea and packed up all our worldly possessions into crates. I can still see the crates even now; they were huge, grainy wooden tea chests that smelt sweetly of light timber. It was strange to see a group of boxes that contained our whole life, stacked neatly side by side.

In those days, people often went around the world by ship. We boarded the SS *Arawa*, a British ship, which was to be our home for almost three months. I haven't really heard of people doing this since then, as three months is a long time, especially while having to do our schoolwork on board. The ship was full of children. After they all embarked, it felt like we had the whole ship to ourselves.

The SS *Arawa* was immense. It had numerous decks and we had a huge cabin on the upper deck. Schoolwork was sparse as there was just too much going on. There were two swimming pools and so many children on board, and we would all be in the pool whenever we could. Dinner was formal. I remember our waiter wearing white gloves and I thought this was quite strange. Breakfast and lunch were the same as dinner: very formal. I found the food a little too exotic at times. I had never heard of eating tongue, which was horrifying for me at that age and is still wedged in my memory.

The staff aboard the *Arawa* kept us busy with games we would all play. You could win prizes, and it was so exciting. It had a massive ballroom, and when we crossed the equator there was a large party there to celebrate. Everyone dressed up in fancy dress. It was a huge competition and you could only make your costume from what you had available.

It was an amazing experience, sailing around on the ocean, pulling into ports in different exotic and amazing countries where we would stay for a day or two, explore and then return. There weren't many ships that did this at that time. Tahiti and Rarotonga were two places we stayed in for a few days, before moving on to other places I had never heard of. We visited Trinidad, where the beaches seemed to go on forever and were people-free. The best thing about visiting different lands was I got to make friends with so many children from different backgrounds and societies.

The children from New Zealand with whom I had made friends disembarked in their homeland after a little while. I had enjoyed their company for at least a month and made a couple of close friends. We

Chapter Two – RETURN TO SYDNEY

docked in New Zealand and took in the amazing sights in this beautiful country and then we continued our ocean journey once again. It was truly an experience of a lifetime, being able to witness each beautiful country. My mum told us not many people get to have that experience, and I thought how lucky I was.

Once we disembarked, we were met by my mum's kind brother and we were once again transported back to Gloucester. I found myself back at 15 Cromwell Street with my aunt and uncle, while my parents decided where they would like to settle and restart their life. It felt like a continuation of our first short visit only a year before; as though we had never left. Cromwell Street was still the same pleasant little street and I was happy to be in my room at the top of the narrow staircase once again.

Chapter Three

GLOUCESTER IN 1970

My parents had all their worldly goods stowed away. Dad bought a smallish car and off we went from place to place with the view to a new and happy life. From picking blackberries along the thin, meandering lanes in Dorset and Cornwall to the excitement of the light show that was the Blackpool Illuminations; Wales, Scotland, and magnificent castles, it felt like we never stopped travelling, but we always ended up back in Gloucester. That was where family were, and of course family was important to my mum and dad.

We would bunker down in 15 Cromwell Street until Mum and Dad would venture to a new place of interest, then off we would go to another tantalising town or hamlet. It felt as though we drove to nearly every settlement there was, meandering through the narrow village streets. We took in all the historical and picturesque sites, magnificent castles and cathedrals. Because I was only ten, it was easy for me to understand my surroundings and adapt to new things I was introduced

Chapter Three – GLOUCESTER IN 1970

to. I fell deeply in love with Gloucester; the people, surroundings and everything about it. It always felt like I was supposed to be living there.

We stayed for six months. It felt like a lot longer to me, but for some reason unknown to me at that time, Mum and Dad couldn't settle, and so we again returned to Sydney. I imagine it was my elastic band theory, pulling them the other way this time.

We flew back to Sydney via America, as my dad's brother had settled in Nevada and started his family. This was a month's stay and a unique experience. My most vivid memory is of Nixon being up for election and the blue badges everyone wore, saying 'Vote for Nixon'. For some reason, even as a ten-year-old, I really wanted one.

We settled back into the Eastern Suburbs of Sydney and Mum and Dad picked up the pieces of their lives and continued as before. We were quite close to the ocean, so life in Sydney was vastly different to England. We would always be at the beach; mornings, afternoon and weekends. Spending time at the beach was a lifestyle, uncrowded and vastly different to what it is now.

So now I had two homes, Gloucester and Sydney, first in the Eastern Suburbs and later the Western Suburbs. I realise now that although we had returned and would never emigrate back to England again as a family, for me the pull was always going to be there. This invisible band now held me firmly within its grip. To what extent it was going to affect my life was unimaginable. I could never imagine that Cromwell Street was going to become a memory for all the wrong reasons.

***

As soon as I turned eighteen, I felt the strong urge to return to England as an adult on a Working Holiday visa. I knew I could easily obtain a secretarial role. I daydreamed of what it would be like to start a new adventure so far away. I decided to pack my things, sell anything and everything I could and fly back to England to live in Gloucester. I could work a little here and there and explore as much of everything and everywhere that I could.

Little did I know this would be a part of my life that would never be far from my memory in ways that I wish I didn't have to think about. It turned out to be a happy and exciting adventure, but came with uncomfortable and frightening experiences that would be forever with me.

It wasn't a quick decision, nor was it a hasty decision to travel to Gloucester. I had a longing to reconnect with family members there as it had been seven or eight years since I had travelled there. I had long held pleasant memories of my stay there when I was a child. I had completed a secretarial course and had managed to find a job close to home. I thought how I could work in different companies and discover new skills in another country. I had the idea that I would have an open ticket and return home when I had learnt enough. It was a thoroughly exciting idea, and it was all I could think about.

I knew that I would have my cousins and other family members around me if I needed them and so I felt completely safe and almost drooling with anticipation. I sold my car, which I knew I wouldn't need for a period of time. I wanted to use the money to help me once I got over there. It was difficult in respect that I was very close to my parents and there was a definite tug at my heartstrings as I told them quietly that I would be going overseas on a working holiday, with no idea when I would be returning. I told them it would be months, not years, and because I was staying with family, they were quite happy with my idea. I left behind a boyfriend who I had been going out with since I was sixteen, but I knew I was nowhere near ready to settle down; I wanted to experience a bit of life before I did that. I did my very best

Chapter Three – GLOUCESTER IN 1970

to make sure my parents knew I would not get into any trouble. Little did I know trouble would find me.

The time had finally arrived. Boarding the plane was a bittersweet. I had said goodbye to all my friends and although I was excited, I still held a quietly nervous feeling within my stomach. I would write to my friends while I was away. This is what we did; there was no internet or Facebook. Not even emails. So we would send these little handwritten blue aerograms back and forth, me outlining my adventures. I missed my friends back home a lot in the first few weeks.

I easily found a small part-time secretarial position in Gloucester Hospital, in the Social Services section. It was only a few days a week, which meant I had the rest of the week to enjoy the sights and sounds of not only Gloucester, but other cities and towns close by—and sometimes quite far away too. Between trips I would return to my aunt and uncle's home and stay a few weeks, giving money to my aunt to pay for the big room I lived in while I was there.

One of my trips was to Jersey, in the Channel Islands. My uncle owned a guesthouse on the island and it was an amazing experience to visit this gorgeous place, steeped in history. It was quiet and the people who lived there were friendly and kind. It is still a strong memory that will stay with me forever; it's always been like a secret island to me. Not many people I have spoken to about it are aware of its existence. Maybe that is a good thing, keep it special.

I found the culture in England was different to Sydney. The scattered pubs were quaint and tucked inside bustling streets which were wonderful places to meet people my own age. Even though I was on my own, I never felt lonely. Strangers would introduce themselves and be interested in where I was from. It seemed everyone flocked to these beautiful little pubs in the evenings after work to relax, keep warm and wind down from a hard day's work. They seemed less rowdy than the pubs back home, and they oozed charm and had an historical feel. I felt I had stepped back in time.

***

I soon made friends and started to make plans to meet up them during the day and on weekends. We did all the things that young people did: shopping, movies and venturing into surrounding towns. My favourite place was Cheltenham. It was not too far away and seemed larger and busier than Gloucester. It came to be one of my favourite places to shop as the shopping centre was open and cheerily inviting, with the community flocking together in groups.

Besides the little pubs, there were two discos in Gloucester. I was told by one of my new friends these were the places to go in the evening to dance and listen to music. You would always meet someone new. Ska and reggae were popular at the time. Whenever I heard those songs for years and years later, I would be right back there again. Reggae didn't seem to be as popular in Australia, but it was huge in England.

I was introduced to Tracy's, a disco tucked in between nondescript buildings. If you blinked, you would surely miss it. I would usually be accompanied by my young uncle, an extremely fun and kind man not much older than me. It would start around nine p.m. and you had to line up to get in; even in winter it was always crowded. The line of patrons would be quite long, with everyone patiently waiting to enter, chattering to each other, with rows of coloured coats, scarves and beanies. Sometimes it was so cold that you could see your breath wavering in front of you. We would huddle together, impatiently waiting to enter, feet shifting to keep our circulation going. Once inside it seemed quite small. You could take off your heavy clothing and not have to be so constrained by it.

Chapter Three – GLOUCESTER IN 1970

I don't recall how much you paid to go inside, but it wouldn't have been too expensive because it was crowded and people were always trying to get in, even after Tracy's had closed its doors. The bar was the near the entrance, there was a dance floor in the middle in front of it, with other bars up the side. It was dark, and it seemed to glow red, maybe from the carpets. There was a small level higher than the dance floor where everybody sat at tables, as well as around the small dance floor.

There would be flashing lights, especially when the dance floor was overflowing. My overall impression from the very first time I entered its doors was of happy, energetic and friendly people, all dancing and smiling. From the outside you could only see a small door with a sign, 'Tracy's', but once inside it was like stepping into another world.

The music was loud and inviting and everyone would be dancing, laughing and having a wonderful time. Everyone seemed to know each other. The feeling inside was absolute excitement, and the beat of the most popular music was always the best treat. It was overwhelming and intoxicating—and I loved every minute of it.

The second disco I was introduced to was Tiffany's, which seemed just the same as Tracy's, but I was told was where the 'toffs' went. Not knowing what 'toffs' meant, I asked and was told it meant more upmarket. At Tracy's you didn't need to dress up too much, which was fine by me. It was jeans and joggers or anything casual. Tiffany's was a very different experience. I enjoyed it, but I did have to dress a little more formally than I would have at Tracy's. It made Tracy's look very small. There was nothing about the venue that stood out as extra special, except that it had a feel of elegance and class; a bit like a debutante ball. The dance floor was huge, and even the security dressed formally.

The people who were there had often been at Tracy's the week before. It seemed everyone went to both. Tracy's was very informal, but at Tiffany's we could all dress up in our clothes that we don't get to wear very often. I found it amusing when I met somebody I'd seen the week before at Tracy's. The music was just the same, reggae and the same famous groups and bands that were all so popular at the time. I felt people were over-dressed, but that was just how it was there and it was a comfortable, classy place to be. I would not have been surprised if someone entered wearing a tiara, that is how beautifully dressed some of the girls were. I tried not to stare but they looked so naturally stunning that it was just like a celebrity event at times.

I was more comfortable going to Tracy's to be honest, and so that was the place I would religiously visit on Fridays and Saturdays, and during the week if it was open. I can't remember what time it closed, but it was always crowded to capacity until the very end. It gave me a feeling of comfort and belonging. I would dance all night, retreating home only when I had exhausted myself. I had never heard of some of the bands and singers that were blaring loudly from massive speakers. England was clearly very ahead of us back home in Australia.

I was still working during the day, or exploring and visiting family when I wasn't, but when I could, I would venture to Tracy's on my own, knowing that I would make new friends and see others I had met only briefly. I didn't visit Tiffany's as often, but I would always have friends that went to both. I knew that I would not be on my own and that I would have people to socialise with.

Chapter Four

MY NEW FRIEND LIZ

One evening while standing in the queue at Tracy's, a new friend introduced me to Liz. Liz was only seventeen, but seemed a lot older. She was tall, statuesque and beautiful. She had brownish hair to her shoulders, flicked up a little at the ends. We started to chat and, like a lot of other people, she enjoyed listening to my Australian accent. It was one of those times when you feel as though you have met the person previously, or they have been in your life before. Almost like walking in the same steps.

I couldn't understand why everyone thought I had an accent—I certainly didn't think I did. Sometimes people would talk to me so I could speak back to them. I remember one girl actually said, 'Gosh, doesn't she speak funny.' This of course made me laugh inside because that is exactly how I thought about everybody else. I thought they spoke funny. I liked to listen to them speak too, as I found the Gloucester accent very pleasant.

Liz told me that she worked behind the bar at Tracy's and that it was one of her nights off. She was wearing a tight skirt that I later found out was called a pencil skirt. It had a little split at the back and was very tight. She had seamed stockings and the highest heels I had ever seen. Most people there were dressed more casually, although some girls did wear pencil skirts. We didn't wear them back home, so I was naturally interested in this new style of dress. They looked smart and glamorous, and I decided I would get one too, although I never did get around to it. I chose to stay in my casual attire of blue jeans and as many jumpers as I could.

Liz and I spoke most of the night, about what I am not sure as it has been so long, but I remember being excited that I had been introduced to her. I didn't know at that time that our friendship would stretch in different ways over decades. We spoke about normal girl stuff, especially boys. She had a kind and gentle voice and she made me laugh incessantly. Through her, I met other people, both boys and girls, and this was when I started to feel settled and my life became busy.

I found out that Liz lived in Cromwell Street too, at number 25, just five doors down, in a bedsit on the top floor. I thought, *What on earth is a bedsit?* We didn't have them back home, not that I knew of. Back home, if you wanted to stay at someone else's house, it would just be a room. I remember thinking how cool it was to have your own little apartment. I told Liz that I was living in my aunt's home at number 15. As it turned out, her mother lived around the corner, although I never met her. I think that is the reason Fred and Rose never touched Liz.

We decided we should meet up during the day when she had time and go shopping or for coffee or lunch, or perhaps clothes hunting. My favourite shop was Debenhams; I could be lost there all afternoon and not even realise it.

Chapter Four – MY NEW FRIEND LIZ

One afternoon, my aunt called from downstairs to say that I had a visitor. My aunt knew all of my cousins and she would have just sent them upstairs to my room. I thought it must be Liz, because no-one besides other family members knew where I was living. I quickly ran down the stairs and showed Liz to my room. We laughed and whispered while devouring cakes and sweets. Everything tasted delicious and decadent, and we prayed we wouldn't feel sick a few hours later. We spoke about the things normal eighteen-year-olds would talk about, just having a pleasant hour or so.

One particular time we were chatting, sitting on my bed, and Liz asked, 'What's your favourite food, Ka,' probably thinking it would be an exotic dish from Australia. I quickly replied, 'Penguins,' as I had just discovered these little biscuits that only England had at that time. We didn't have them back home. They were delicious, just chocolate biscuits with cream in the middle, nothing extra special, but I was quietly addicted to them.

Liz looked absolutely horrified. Her face crumpled like a brown paper bag, she went pale and whispered in a tone of shock and horror, 'You eat penguins. Well, how do you eat them? Do you bake them?' I giggled. I knew from her face alone that she thought I was talking about cooking real-life penguins. 'No', I said, 'they're chocolate biscuits over here. They are so nice. I can't stop eating them. I've got them stored in my bedside drawer. We don't have them back home.' With that, we both collapsed into laughter, laughing so much I thought I was going to be sick. It still is one of the funniest moments in my life. Whenever I see a penguin, I am taken back to that memory of us giggling on the bed all those decades ago.

Chapter Five

MEETING FRED AND ROSE: STEPPING INTO THE WEB

It was a winter morning when Liz came over and said, 'Hey, Ka, do you want to come to my bedsit while I grab some things and we can go out for a while?' I said, 'Sure,' and off we went. It was only just down the street, exactly five houses down. It looked like all the other houses and I was curious to peer inside. I'm not a stickybeak by nature, but the houses here were unique and different, and I enjoyed visiting these lovely warm and inviting homes.

Number 25 felt as though it was at the end of the street, but I'm not absolutely sure. I heard that the house has been pulled down, which is a good thing. I stood outside looking up at the top windows with their green frames and Liz pointed to her room, which was on the right at the top of the three rows of windows. The building itself was a dirty cream colour and with its green windowsills, the house stood out from the others on Cromwell Street. There was a little concrete path leading

Chapter Five – MEETING FRED AND ROSE: STEPPING INTO THE WEB

up to the heavy, dark-coloured door. It didn't seem very large from the outside, but once inside it seemed big, with a steep staircase visible on entering the front door. There was a small veranda that you would walk across, which I heard later was where the bodies were buried. There was no front garden that I noticed.

The door was open and we entered to see a roughly dressed man standing right in front of us. It was Fred. He was hammering at the timber of the stair banister, but he stopped when we came inside. Rose was near the open doorway next to him, and she left quickly after a brief introduction. She seemed to be in a hurry, although she smiled when we were introduced. I think she was rushing out the door at the time, going somewhere. She wore glasses, and I was a little taken aback because they were almost identical to my mother's. Maybe that fact made me feel as though I could be safe around her. Looks are deceiving and in this case, her quiet demeanour hid the horrific and depraved acts she performed upon young women.

Fred was not that tall, and a bit chubby if I remember right. His face was a little grubby and he had bushy, untidy eyebrows. I thought he looked unkempt. He was wearing an old baggy greenish jumper with holes in it, and it was obvious he was dressed to do jobs around the house. His hands were roughish and covered in dirt, which made me think he was a builder. He looked at me from top to toe, said nothing, and then continued hammering. Liz introduced me and I can still hear her words. 'Hey, Fred, this is Ka. She is visiting from Australia.'

Still hammering, he stopped for the briefest moment, looked at me again and asked quietly and slowly, 'And where are you living luv?' I can still hear the words. He gave me a quiet sense of unease and I wondered why he would ask something like that. It gave me a chill and I remember the hairs rising on my arms and legs. My spine had a chill vehemently embedded within it. I wanted to be respectful, as he was the owner of the house and I was in his home, so I nervously replied, 'Five doors down at number 15, with my aunt and uncle.' As soon as I said that I felt his demeanour change. His body shifted and he stiffened a little. It was only for a brief second and it didn't mean much then, but I did notice it. His attitude to me was one of total dismissal and I felt he wanted me to leave. The uneasiness I felt was something I couldn't explain. There was no reason I should feel that way, but all the same, I had a great desire to rush past him and run up to Liz's bedsit. I remember standing close to him while my feet shifted from one to the other nervously, a nervousness that I could not explain.

I can still hear his words, asking where I lived—it's funny how a few words stay with you. I think that because he knew I lived down the road, and with my family, he couldn't do anything to me. He knew my aunt and uncle too, so I was of no use to him. Everyone says, 'Oh, they just kept to themselves'. I don't think that's true, because my aunt and uncle knew them as neighbours and were perfectly happy for me to move into their home with Liz on my return to Gloucester in 1979.

I heard decades later that girls who rented and lodged there, usually four at a time, were often homeless and had nowhere else to stay. They were all my age. No-one asked questions about them, but my family would be asking. Liz had lived there for quite a while, at least seven years, and her mum lived around the corner.

After the uncomfortable introduction had thankfully come to an end, I was glad to be out of Fred West's sight. As we climbed the stairs, I could hear subtle noises behind the doors on the way up. It seemed to be a busy place with lodgers coming and going; a quiet bustling of different people entering and exiting the house.

My legs were jelly as I plodded up the stairs as quickly as I could. It was more than one flight, and the steep stairs creaked with each step. There was a strange smell downstairs that I couldn't put my finger

Chapter Five – MEETING FRED AND ROSE: STEPPING INTO THE WEB

on. It wasn't a smell you could really relate to anything in particular and I don't know if anybody else smelt what I did. I passed it off as a cooking smell, but I now know it wasn't. It was an unusual, unpleasant, sickly smell that I had never smelt before.

I decided not to be rude and say anything about this stench. Each time I visited Liz or came down from her bedsit, the same smell would be wafting up the staircase and lingering around the bottom floor. It actually smelt worse on the ground floor and as I got further upstairs, it petered out.

Karen's father in his pilot uniform, WW2.

This is a never-before seen photo of Aung San, the founding father of Burma and the real-life father of democracy icon Aung San Suu Kyi. Karen's father was Aung San's personal pilot in 1947.

10-year-old Karen on the bridge of the SS Arawa, a British ship, 1969.

Karen having fun in Tredworth, Gloucester, at 18-years-old on her first solo trip.

20-year-old Karen at a party.

Karen as a 20-year-old in Sydney.

20-year-old Karen with her mum and dad and Penny the poodle in their backyard in the Blue Mountains.

Karen's long-lost friend, Liz, whom she never met up with again, and will keep in her heart forever.

Illustration by Karen's son, Dane.

Chapter Six

THE BEDSIT

The bedsit on the top floor was inviting and always warm. When I first entered, sun was streaming through the one window that opened onto the street. It seemed quite spacious, although I know it wasn't. It was probably the way Liz set it out, with two single beds and a table. She had a little cooktop outside the bedsit; small, but very convenient, and a small fridge where we stashed our sugary snacks. We ate a lot of junk, and as an 18-year-old, you just stay skinny. We didn't really cook that much, if I remember rightly. Our hours made it difficult to schedule regular meals, and we were out a lot. Everyone we hung around with was under twenty or just over; not a prime age for cooking. I think we all just wanted to have lots of fun, go places and do things.

But I do remember thinking how cool the little kitchen area was. It was just large enough for one or two people. There was a room directly opposite Liz's, so I suppose the lodger in that room used it too. Either way, it was super convenient when we didn't want to go out on bleak days when the temperature was freezing. The house had no communal area.

Chapter Six – THE BEDSIT

Liz's bedsit faced the street, so I couldn't see the narrow back garden that held such dreadful secrets. But I remember a door being open one day, and I caught a glimpse of it, the long, thin garden that would become a burial ground.

We would both lean from the front window that looked out onto the street and chat with friends on the pavement below. On various occasions there would be a group of us, boys and girls, outside, yelling up and down to each other from the window to the pavement. We used to have a lot of fun socialising this way, although I don't think we did this in winter. Sometimes the ice on the pavement would be quite a deterrent to bantering outside.

Liz's room felt homely and safe from the outside world and the cold, although I now know that was not the case at all. The bathroom, however, made me uneasy. It is difficult to remember it in detail, but believe it was just one floor down from Liz's room; the shower was somewhere else. It was very small; just a toilet and a sink, really, and it was all metal. I distinctly remember feeling uncomfortable and I definitely didn't want to be in there. I don't know exactly why I was uneasy in this bathroom area, but it was definitely a feeling of get in and get out as quickly as you can.

I didn't like going up and down the stairs to and from the bedsit at night. I used to run up the stairs behind Liz. I still remember seeing her joggers in front of my face. I ran up as fast as I could behind her, unable to shake the feeling that somebody else was behind me.

But in spite of that creepy bathroom and the stairs that gave me inexplicable chills, I thought how lucky Liz was, independent and enjoying her own little domain. She could do whatever she wanted and the independence she obtained from this bedsit was, to me, fantastic. I wished I could have my own bedsit.

I would visit Liz when whenever I could, almost daily. I would knock on a large door at the side of the house, and often Rose West would tell me that Liz was upstairs and let me go straight up to her room. I found Rose to be very polite and quietly spoken, but she always made me feel uncomfortable, and I didn't want to be in her company. She basically scared me a little, with no reason why; I just felt the undercurrent of not wanting to be in her presence for too long. Little did I know there really was a reason I felt uncomfortable around her, and the reason shocked and horrified me decades later. It took a huge amount of time to find out why I felt scared of this bespectacled, homely-looking woman.

I would continue going to Tracy's and sometimes met up with Liz, but most times she was behind the bar. I would wait for her to finish her shift and we would then walk home together. I walked to number 15 Cromwell Street and went upstairs to my room, and she would continue down the road to number 25. It went on like that for a short while.

One evening on arriving at Tracy's I saw Liz at the front of the queue, as it was her night off. She had dyed her hair very light blonde and it looked fantastic. Now she reminded me of Marilyn Monroe. I was in total awe. After dancing around for a while and just being joyful as only teenagers can, with lots of people we knew, she asked if I wanted to work behind the bar too. I had just finished up in a secretarial role and I was free to take up her offer.

I looked at her with a confused smile. I said, 'I've never done that before. I don't know what to do.' She grinned and stated matter-of-factly that the manager at Tracy's was a very nice person and she would talk to him. Maybe I could get trained and start pouring lager and spirits. I must admit I was very interested, as it looked fun and we could work together. I was keen for a totally new experience. I thought how I could work in the evenings and travel around during the day, which in theory was a great idea, but it didn't turn out like that at all.

Chapter Six – THE BEDSIT

***

It worked. The manager said yes and the next evening I started my new role as a barmaid. Once behind the bar, I was introduced to the very tall and exotic African lady who was in charge. I was a little intimidated by her, but I had no need to be. She navigated me through everything I had to do to be a barmaid. If I was stuck with an order for a drink that I had no idea existed or was not confident with pouring, she was there to assist.

I was shown how to pour lager, lager and lime, and lager with lemonade, and spirits that I had never heard of before. The bar served pints or half-pints. Back home we had schooners and middies, so this was a totally new concept. Once I began my first shift, I realised how difficult it was going to be. Being a barmaid was harder than I thought. I had lager going all over the place, pouring onto the floor, my shoes, and even my hair and my clothes. I was lucky everyone seemed oblivious to the excess liquid that went onto the tiles beneath our feet. I quickly realised it was a very, very fast-paced role. I have never been a drinker and the spirits were tricky as I had never even heard of some of them. A lot of them were French, or from other European countries. This is when I first discovered Pernod.

The shift lasted about six hours. By the end of the night, the floor was grimy and sticky and my feet stuck on the tacky tiles and made a squishy sound every time I walked. At the end of the shift I felt grimy and my clothes stank of lager. They were evenings of physical exertion and the never-ending pouring of alcohol, as well as chatting to the hundreds of patrons that would flock to the bar. There would usually be a line three patrons deep, and I was running around, up and down all night. It is one of the hardest physical jobs I have ever done. Liz and I would sometimes meet up in pubs like Lemon & Parker, which had been there since the 1900s and seemed very classy. It was huge, the first city centre pub with a balcony. At the back was a popular disco. It was close to the Gloucester Guildhall and we loved it there.

Being a barmaid was an amazing way to meet more and more young people my own age. We seemed to make many friends over time, both male and female. We didn't really get time to have boyfriends, although I know that Liz met her future husband sometime after I had returned home, and had four children with him. I didn't even get to meet him, but he was the love of her life. I was always so busy, and probably too overwhelmingly distracted by my new life. A boyfriend would have been a huge development in my solo jaunt, but thinking back, I was just far too engulfed in travelling, working and being overwhelmed by excitement and happiness. I now feel relieved that I didn't have a boyfriend, as it would have been terrifying for him to discover the truth about that house.

I continued working as a barmaid for quite a few months. One evening, Liz suggested, 'Hey, Ka, why don't you sleep at my place after work in the evenings when we have shifts? You wouldn't wake up your aunt or uncle. We can go to work the next evening together.' I had been thinking about this, as I always worried that my trudging up the three flights of stairs in the wee hours of the morning would wake my aunt or uncle. They were elderly and it was always very important to me that I respected them by being quiet late at night.

We didn't finish until two in the morning, or sometimes even later, and by the time I got home, it was very, very late. Every step on the stairs sounded amplified. I had mentioned this to Liz, saying how I tried to be quiet when I got home but the stairs creaked. I said would think about this idea and speak to my aunt and uncle. I was only eighteen and I wanted to make sure they would be okay with this too.

Chapter Six – THE BEDSIT

After a while, I took up Liz's offer. I moved a lot of my clothes there, so I didn't go back to 15 Cromwell Street much. I always visited family during the daytime and spent the evenings working, and now I didn't have to feel guilty for waking my aunt and uncle while I was a barmaid with crazy shifts. I found bar work exhausting, but still fun and exciting. Bed always seemed a welcoming sight after a gruelling evening of running up and down the sticky floor while frantically pouring lager.

Every night after Tracy's closed, we would go to a Chinese restaurant nearby called Ken's. I have heard it is still there all these decades later, although I can't be certain. It was on the way home, and we would walk there. It was always open; it would be three in the morning and we would eat and chat about the evening for another half-hour or so. This was our nighttime ritual, with the food being particularly delicious. We were ravenous after a busy shift and our young bodies needed sustenance. Afterwards we would stumble home and sleep the deepest sleep possible. We would crash with exhaustion and sleep the whole day until it was time to go back to work for another round of pouring alcohol. This is how I started staying with Liz in her bedsit at number 25 Cromwell Street after our shifts.

I didn't feel comfortable on my first night there. It was Spring, but there was a feeling of heaviness in the house. The stairs seemed to go on forever. It was my first night in a strange house and I thought all first nights were creepy. I felt a coldness that lifted when I reached Liz's room.

In the darkness of the early mornings, 25 Cromwell Street felt eerie when we returned to sleep after our evening shift. It was quiet, but an uncomfortable and creepy quiet. The strange, lingering odour was always present. It seemed to permeate all the way to the top of the stairs, but was not as strong by the time I reached the top. I would crumple my nose so that I couldn't smell it as I rushed up to Liz's bedsit.

I was grateful when we reached the top floor and entered Liz's room to sleep.

We would crawl out of bed, have something to eat and then go straight to Tracy's for our evening shift. Fairly soon it felt as though we were vampires—sleeping during the day and only going out in the dark. After a while, my face turned pale from seeing no sunlight during the day. I just wanted to sleep all day and not venture outside. The evenings were so adrenaline-soaked and energy-sucking that sleep was a craving after a week of gruelling shifts.

My aunt had decided that I didn't need to pay her any board as I was only there a few days or nights a week and the rest of my time was spent with Liz. From that time, I would give Liz a small amount, the detail of which I can't remember, and that would help pay her rent to Fred and Rose. It was such a great idea, because most of waking life and time away from work was spent here.

Liz told me about the children living there, Rose and Fred's children. I knew that she was fond of them. She spoke often about Heather, Fred's and Rose's daughter. I remember thinking how quiet the children were. I only saw them briefly during my period of stay. I thought they were the most well-behaved children, only soft noises coming from behind closed doors and never any fighting. In the evenings there would be muffled noises behind each solid door as you went up the stairs, or maybe a television playing.

I saw the children very rarely as our working hours made it difficult to see anybody in the house. I didn't hear them at all in the late evenings or early mornings after a shift. They were most probably asleep. I can still remember how small and innocent they always looked. Whenever I saw them, they seemed to be wearing black, and I wonder now if that was their school uniform. They were always neatly dressed and I remember they had shortish hair. They really did look alike. Liz would talk about the two girls, and especially Heather. She would say how she had spoken to her one day or had done something with her, or for them both. She always praised the girls. She really adored them. There were other children living in the house, but Liz seemed to be closer to these two sweet young girls. I loved to see them around the house, too. They seemed to lighten the dreary surroundings and cold energy that prevailed.

I didn't find out until decades later that three of their children were actually sleeping in the cellar while we walked above them, with the bodies of girls buried beneath the concrete while the Wests slept and we were upstairs. I was horrified to realise that that was why they were so quiet. My skin crawls when I think of how we knew nothing of what was going on at that time. It was not the kind of thing you would even think was happening while you rushed through your working life.

You could sometimes hear doors opening and shutting, which I assumed was the other lodgers coming and going. If I ever passed an open door, I would try to peer in and see what the other rooms were like. They were just plain rooms, nothing more than that, nondescript in every way, and this is where homeless girls would pay money to stay. The rooms looked large, like Liz's, and sparse, with just a bed and other smallish bits of furniture. It had the feel of a very chaotic house with the hustle and bustle of people going about their lives. Now, I too was a part of that chaos.

I enjoyed seeing people coming and going. One or two of the girls would always greet me. I had no time to be lonely. The rooms I saw besides Liz's were on the other side of the house, facing the back. I knew they looked over the backyard and I noticed sunlight coming through one of the rooms when I briefly glanced inside.

When we came home from our shift, we crept up the stairs as quietly as possible, our feet always creaking on every step. Every creak made me cringe, and each sounded twice as loud as it actually was. I didn't like those stairs at all. They seemed to be a little unstable and so steep. The creaking seemed to be exacerbated at night. You didn't really hear the creaking during daylight hours. The house was noisy during the day whenever I was there. In the evenings you could sometimes hear soft voices behind closed doors, muffled sounds or laughter.

Everything seemed ordinary, but there was that foreboding smell that made you run up the stairs as fast as you could, and the energy, particularly centred downstairs, held a feeling of oppression and heaviness. It was as though the air was heavy. This was particularly strong when I entered the front door, as well as on the lower floor. The downstairs always felt much colder than the upper part of the house. I had this intense desire to bolt up the stairs to Liz's bedsit as fast as my legs could carry me, to warmth. I didn't want to be downstairs; it just didn't feel comfortable at all.

During the day Liz's bedsit felt like more than just one room. The window had a fine cotton curtain draped in front of it, and the sun always shone in the mornings, warming up the room for the entire day. The two single beds were on either side of the room and although I don't remember exactly where the wardrobe was, the room was always neat and spotless. Our clothes were always stored neatly away. The winters were a new experience for me, having had sunshine and mild winters all my life. Liz's room would be bright and warm. I'm sure she had a heater of some sort, but it wasn't a particularly large room, so it didn't take much to warm it.

One door on the left, close to the front door if I remember rightly, was a silvery colour, or a metal of some sort. It looked a little odd melded into an old wall. This door looked relatively new, the patterned metal quite shiny. It had a lock on it. I remember thinking that it looked strange and ominous, like it held a secret. It wasn't as tall as a

Chapter Six – THE BEDSIT

normal-sized door and it looked thinner than most doors. I wondered why it had a lock firmly intact on the outside. I wondered who had the key. I knew I would never venture behind it. The house looked as though it was under renovation in places, so a newly placed door was no surprise. I dismissed it from my mind and carried on with my busy schedule.

One day, as we were slipping outside into the cold for lunch at the Cromwell Pub, Liz pointed to the door and said, 'Ka, Fred said we can't go in this door under any circumstances.' I thought, *Well, fine, I have no intention of going in*, but I quietly said, 'Okay, I wonder what it is?' We both thought it looked strange. I asked a little inquisitively, 'Do you think it's a bathroom?' Liz said she had no idea. I told her I wouldn't be going in there. I told her how weird it looked. We looked at each other at the same time and both shrugged. We didn't discuss it again. It was just always there at the bottom of the stairs, tempting us to enter. I remember feeling slightly uncomfortable when I glanced at it quickly any time that I passed it. Whenever anyone says you can't enter somewhere or something, I wonder why. It makes me want to know more. But not with this door. Something inside of me said to stay away, and so I did. I heard later that it went to the cellar, where Fred and Rose committed unspeakable crimes. We had made a pact not to not enter, and I'm extremely grateful for that life-saving decision made all those years ago. If I close my eyes, I can still see the out-of-place door in front of me.

The house, with its subtle, sickening, strange odour, gave off a feel of chaos. I used to wonder if Liz smelt it too, but I never said anything. I thought maybe I was imagining it, even though it was the same every time I was there. It never changed and never went away.

There seemed to be a lot more people entering the house than lived there, and I used to think that Rose and Fred had many visitors. Often when I would be entering the heavy door to go upstairs to see Liz, there would be one or two people passing by to go about their business of daily life, or maybe visiting. The house seemed to hum with activity, with all the different people entering and leaving. I was a guest as far as I was concerned, even though I gave Liz a little money for my time spent there. I always made sure I was respectful to Fred and Rose and the other lodgers whenever I came in contact with them. I wanted to be friendly with everyone. I was meeting new people in my new life and I was eager and excited to socialise.

Sometimes days in England can be dark and seem melancholy, especially when there is a steady, cold drizzle outside, but this wasn't what made the house dark. It was something entirely different. Whatever it was, it made the hair on my arms stand on end. Even though it was a nondescript terrace house by all accounts, it felt unique. Not every house in the street rented out their spare rooms, and I thought it was a fantastic idea. Most of the lodgers were my age, I was told. They had no family or home life, and this was a haven for them. Of course, this haven did not exist. With so many lodgers and the quite large West family ensconced on the lower floor, the house had a pulse of its very own.

I would often see Fred hanging around outside the house, usually with a hammer in his hand, looking scruffy and downtrodden. He always had messy hair with the same old baggy clothes and often he would be in the same raggedy jumper. I knew he had no interest in me, but I still passed him as speedily as my feet would carry me. if he saw me, I would sometimes say a quiet hello, only because I had to, but I usually tried to not let him see me. It was like playing the Artful Dodger, not letting him see you so you didn't have to talk. There was something about him that made me nervous. If I saw him drive off down the road, I would scamper up to see Liz before he came back and saw me.

Chapter Six – THE BEDSIT

Liz was quite fond of him, not knowing anything of his murderous ways, and thought he was just a little offbeat or strange. I can remember her telling me that she had asked Fred if it was okay for me to stay with her upstairs in her bedsit because we were working together and it was more convenient for us both. She told me that he had been more than happy. I can remember her telling me how odd he was, but not to be nervous about him. She told me that he came across as gruff at times. She told me how Rose was a bit simple, but that she was harmless too. I wasn't sure what 'simple' meant, but I found Rose to be quiet and unassuming, although at times I could hear her voice very loud and sharp. I knew that Liz sometimes had tea and dinner and attended social events in the home and I cannot even contemplate how the shock of the discovery of her friends and Heather would have been for her. I knew that Liz was very attached to Fred and Rose and their children. She loved them.

I had no idea of his murderous ways or his depraved acts upon young women in the time I spent there. The fact that Liz told me they were safe, just odd, made me feel that they were just a normal Gloucester family. I had no idea that lodgers were going missing. Liz used to tell me when someone moved out. I didn't seem to see them that often at all, anyway. My new lifestyle was taken up with work and I was only awake at night. There was only the daytime and that is when our hibernation started, so to speak.

I sometimes wonder what could have happened to me if circumstances were different, if my family members weren't living five doors down the road; if I had no-one, like the innocent girls who were tortured and murdered. If my aunt and uncle didn't live down the road, would Fred or Rose have drugged and tortured me too? His skin was a bit rough I thought, maybe from being outside in the cold, and he used to grin a lot. It wasn't the best, most flattering grin, and I felt I had to be wary of him. When I think about them now, it felt like they were both spiders and we were the flies. Fred had a strong, heavy vibration around him, and I felt it was not good to go near him when I was without Liz.

Even though Liz had said that they were a lovely, if slow, couple, I got the distinct feeling that she thought of them as extended family. Liz was happy living at the top of the house. I liked it too. She had told me that she was very settled. She once said, 'Ka, Fred and Rose are really nice, but you have to watch Fred.' She giggled when she said this. I told her that I would be very careful and laughed with her.

Chapter Seven

GOSSIP

One evening Liz and I were walking back from a quaint old pub called the Wellington Arms, which has now been converted into a convenience store. It was a cool, crisp evening and the lights behind the terrace windows were dimming for the evening, chatter echoing from behind the glass. Families were watching television or washing up after dinner, generally retiring for the evening. There was a cool breeze. Cromwell Street was close by and we spoke a little while we walked.

Out of the blue, Liz made a bizarre statement. She spoke quietly, a little secretively. 'Ka, everyone is talking about Rose, it's going around the neighbourhood.' I can still hear her words echoing in my mind and her statement that has haunted me up until this time. The only sound I could hear were our shoes tapping on the road as we walked along, just Liz and me with no-one else in the street. I longed to reach my bed and sleep. I wasn't thinking of anything in particular when Liz's words completely stunned me.

When I asked her what it was, she replied, 'They say Rose is a prostitute and has lots of Black men coming to the house for sex. They say Fred knows, and he takes all the money. They make loads of money. They say he encourages it.' My hand covered my mouth, quietening a gasp, and I said, 'Really? Do you think it's true?' She answered, in a quiet, knowing voice, 'Well, I see lots of Black men coming in and out all the time. They all go and see Rose. So maybe it is true. I see a lot of men, not just a few.'

That is all she said, her words soft as though it was a secret; gossip that was not meant for anyone else's ears. We both burst into giggles at the thought of it, and I said, 'You know, in twenty years' time we will write a book about how Rose was a prostitute and she and Fred murdered people.'

We didn't believe this at all; Liz was just telling me what she had heard. I did see men in the stream of people coming and going, but I didn't think anything of it, although there were no male lodgers at the house on Cromwell Street as far as I know.

I was not aware that our conversation would turn out to be so prophetic and it would turn out to be all true. The awful secret was bandied about all those years ago, decades before their horrendous murders were brought to light.

We reached Liz's bedsit and fell asleep and we never spoke about it again. It was just a random conversation after all, one that could never be true. But Liz noticed all the men coming and going and told me how a few girls had moved out of the house and she hadn't seen them again. Soon I started to notice men coming and going at odd times. We still didn't think it was anything sinister, but as they say, where there's smoke, there's fire. If I had known what atrocities were occurring, I would have run away as fast as I could.

Chapter Seven – GOSSIP

***

After about eleven months, I began thinking about going home. It started with a gnawing homesickness for my family back home and missing all my old friends. My adventure was still enjoyable, and being a barmaid was still fun, but there was a slight nagging feeling of wanting to return. My homesickness for Australia would not dissipate and I pondered returning home once and for all. Although I was enjoying my new life with new friends and wonderful family in Gloucester, the pull was too great. I began to make plans to get things in motion.

I eventually booked a one-way ticket to Sydney and started packing. Saying goodbye to family and friends, and especially Liz, gave me such an awful feeling inside and it was done with a lot of sadness. Liz came with me to the airport with loads of boxes and a couple of suitcases full of the possessions I'd accumulated in my time there. Liz had to take some back and my aunt had to ship them to Sydney. Saying goodbye to Liz and a couple of other close friends before I boarded my plane is the saddest memory of my time there. Leaving England for Australia was a bittersweet moment. I was comforted by the thought that knew I would go back again.

We promised to write to each other. Back then there was no email, no Facebook, no internet, so it was just handwritten letters. And we did write to each other. I would anxiously wait for a letter or an aerogram and tear it open as I hastily read the scrawling writing, taking in every word. There were no phone calls, although I am not sure why not. Maybe it was too expensive back then.

I was nineteen by this time and I had to pick up my life again after my adventure of a lifetime. I soon found a secretarial role in Sydney and reconnected with my old friends. It had only been a year, but it seemed as though I had been away a lot longer. I couldn't settle at all. Everything felt uncomfortable and I kept thinking of everyone back in Gloucester and how I missed them, like I belonged there and not in Australia anymore. I felt like I didn't fit in with my Australian life. This feeling went on for quite a while. I did my best to continue where I had left off before I went, and tried my hardest to be happy. There was always that strong pull between Gloucester and Australia. I felt an intense desire to return to Gloucester again, even if for a short visit.

I decided to save up and go over to visit Liz, family, and other people I had met. That that is exactly what I did. After a year of saving, and now aged twenty, I sold my car and all my worldly goods and bought a return ticket to Heathrow. I started planning my visit, feverishly excited at the very thought of returning.

Chapter Eight

THE RETURN TO GLOUCESTER

It was 1979 when I returned once again to 15 Cromwell Street, anticipating the continuation of a happy holiday and ready for a short adventure. The Winter of Discontent was behind us, and Margaret Thatcher was elected prime minister in May.

I hurriedly unpacked my bags and travelled around Gloucester to visit my family members, including my grandmother. That is when I thought of how my parents must have felt, being pulled between Gloucester and Australia. Two places, always thinking of one when in the other. I only had four weeks there this time and I had to fit in a lot of visits. It felt like I had never left, to be honest. It was as though everything was just the same and the intervening year had not even happened. I was so excited to be settled in my other home.

As soon as I had the time, I scurried down to Liz's bedsit at the top of number 25, almost tripping over my own shoelaces in anticipation. She knew I was coming as I had written to her weeks before, and I wondered if she was as excited as I was. I walked through the old gate and knocked on the door. I stood for a while, but there was no answer. I used to sometimes go through the door without knocking, but I didn't feel good about doing that now as it had been too long. I waited a couple of minutes and knocked a few more times, but there was still no answer. Disappointed, I turned around and plodded heavily towards the gate. I asked myself if I should stay longer and knock again. But by this time, I already had one foot outside the gate. Then I heard a voice behind me and the heavy creak of the door opening.

'Can I help you?' I turned to see Rose standing in the doorway in a flowing black skirt. She had those same large black glasses I had seen her wear before, the ones that looked like my mum's.

I said, 'I'm Karen from Australia, I wonder if I could see Liz please.' She said Liz was at her mum's and would be back later. I was hoping she remembered me, but she didn't give any sign that she recognised me from the year before. There were two of the prettiest little girls standing either side of her, hiding behind her billowing skirt. They seemed shy, and amused by my accent. They looked to be about ten years old, and at first I thought they were twins. Their large, questioning eyes peered at me from behind Rose's black skirt, obviously wondering who I was. I smiled, because they looked so sweet and I wanted them to not be afraid of me. I had only briefly met them the year before and although I had seen them around the house, I knew they didn't recognise me. I used to think what well-behaved children they were, only hearing their voices in the front room to the left when walking through the front door. I found out decades later that these two sweet little girls were Heather, who was killed by Fred, and her sister, Mae. There were other children that lived there, but it is Heather and Mae who haunt my memories.

'Okay, I will come back later,' I said. Rose then asked sweetly, 'Would you like to come in for a cup of tea and wait for her? She shouldn't be

Chapter Eight – THE RETURN TO GLOUCESTER

too long.' Her voice sounded kind and soft, and very inviting. I looked at her and thought maybe I should, as I was quite partial to a cup of tea. I was about to say yes when all of a sudden I heard bells and chimes, high-pitched and loud. I then heard voices say, 'She's too nice, she's too nice.'

As soon as I heard these chimes and voices, something told me not to accept her invitation. The voices were piercingly loud, and the only words were, 'She's too nice.' The voices said these words over and over without a break, until I stopped walking towards the door. I turned around and looked right and then left, and even turned around a little, but there was nobody anywhere to be seen. It felt like the voices came from somewhere else and I just knew it meant not to go in there and that there was a definite danger to my wellbeing. The hairs on my arms stood up on end and I felt freezing cold. I just knew I was not safe.

A shiver went down my spine as I stared at Rose in the doorway. The freezing cold didn't last for long and the chimes and voices ceased, but it was enough for me to not continue. I felt nauseous and a little dizzy. I wasn't terrified, but I felt an urge to keep my distance from Rose. I now believe with all certainty that those chimes saved my life, because if it weren't for them I think I would have gone inside. I said, 'No, it's okay, I will come back later,' I turned and hurried off back to number 15 and the safety of my room at the top of the stairs.

***

I never told anyone about the voices of warning, nor the bells and chimes. I kept it to myself for decades and even now it is bewildering. I still wonder where the voices came from.

I was born a twin but my twin sister, Debbie, died at six months. Maybe that's what made me hear voices, chimes and bells. Maybe she protected me. No-one has ever been able to explain that, but I think that maybe she is like a guardian angel, warning me of the danger that might be coming my way. Revealing my supernatural experiences is difficult, because people laugh at you. I had an aunt, my dad's sister, who was a clairvoyant, the best one you'd ever get. Everyone made fun of her, and she moved to get away from them. So I think it's in the family. My dad told me we come from gypsies.

I am so glad I didn't take up Rose's offer of a cup of tea. Decades later I heard that Rose used to manipulate young women to have tea and then drug them, dragging them down into the cellar, where she and Fred would do unspeakable things to their victims. I am quite partial to a good cup of tea, but this is one that I am glad I did not indulge in.

***

A few hours later, Liz came to 15 Cromwell Street, where I was once again staying with my aunt and uncle while I visited, and we continued our friendship like there had never been a year's gap. It was as if I had never been gone. I spent the next four weeks hanging out with Liz and a couple of her friends, just doing a little bit of shopping here and there, especially in Cheltenham, and of course venturing into London on the train. This is almost fifty years ago now, and it wasn't as built up or as busy as it is now, but it was still just as exciting. It was a fabulous four weeks, catching up with family and friends, and even making new ones. I had and still have cousins and other family living in Gloucester and five decades ago there were even more than there are now.

I still thought Liz's bedsit was the best thing ever. I felt at home again and that this was my other home on the other side of the world. I had lived on Cromwell Street, on and off, since I was ten. I had this feeling that I didn't want to ever leave again.

Chapter Nine

MEETING SHIRLEY ROBINSON

The encounters I had with the other young lodgers were numerous but ever so brief, as I was usually coming in or going out, running up the stairs or just hanging around the front door, waiting for Liz. I remember seeing one of the lodgers being interviewed after the crimes were revealed, and I was quite taken back as I recognised her face.

One new friend who I met through Liz was a young lady called Shirley Robinson. Our introduction was an out-of-this-world experience that was frightening and has caused me great bewilderment. I have never quite understood what happened, but I do know much more now about why I had the experience in that room, Liz's room.

It was a week before I was due to return home. Shirley knocked on Liz's door, and Liz introduced me. She told me that Shirley was another boarder living in Fred and Rose West's home. She said that Shirley was a really gentle and quiet girl whom she had met when she moved in. Shirley was not short, but not tall either and had big, brown, soulful eyes and brownish hair. She was wearing grey trackpants and I thought she looked pregnant, maybe only three to four months. I quickly dismissed that thought. It was just an observation, and I wouldn't ask. I said hello to her and our eyes seemed to lock together. It was as though her eyes bored into mine.

I had the most overwhelming and frightening feeling of absolute hatred from her. Or what I thought then was hatred. It was like an electric shock. It only lasted a second, but it upset me greatly because I was thinking, *she hates me, but why, what I have done?* It was the strongest energy I have ever experienced and I wasn't even sure what it was. All I could ask myself was why she hated me so much. It confused me for a second. The energy that lingered around her made me feel frightened.

Our eyes connected for a brief moment. All of a sudden, I was thrown back against the wall behind me, although not in the physical sense. Bang! I hit the wall, and it hurt. But my body hadn't moved, not my physical body, that is. This was happening the whole time I was looking at Shirley, while we were standing in a little group near the door to the bedsit. I hadn't moved, but some part of me had. It felt like the wind had been knocked out of me. I couldn't breathe for a brief second. I remember feeling nauseous and frightened, not sure what had happened. I didn't know at the time that the feeling I thought was hatred was far worse than hatred. I didn't understand any of this until decades later. I knew this was a very strange experience, but for some reason I never delved into it.

I was glad that no-one had noticed. I kept talking and looking at Shirley the whole afternoon, all the time wondering why she hated me so much. I was back in my body again and still pondering what was going on. I felt like I was dying. Shirley had somehow connected with me. I didn't know if she felt anything; I was in a bit of shock. It was like Shirley and I were in a little bubble of our own, no-one else, just Shirley and me. It is still to this day the highest degree of fear, primal and intense, that I have ever experienced, and I will never forget it. To this very day, decades later, it haunts me, and I can still take myself straight back there if I choose to. I choose not to think of this experience as I am instantly taken back and I feel sick in the stomach. What happened is still with me. I know now that she was terrified. She was not really smiling.

I can still remember when I said goodbye to her. I can still see her face and recall that feeling she gave me, it was a haunting sadness that came off her. I wonder now if it was some sort of premonition, because I know she was murdered by Fred West soon after that.

***

I found out decades later from Liz that a heavily pregnant Shirley had been strangled by Fred West in Liz's room, right where we were standing, in the same place that I felt as if I was thrown against the wall. Her body and that of her unborn child, which was Fred's, were found in the back garden in 1994. To this day I sometimes feel guilty because I didn't know how terrified she was. I didn't pick up on it. Maybe I could have helped.

***

After that eerie and supernatural experience, we talked and hung out in Liz's room. Another lodger from downstairs drifted up a little later. It was a pleasant afternoon, but I was exhausted by my strange experience. After a while I said goodbye as Shirley left and retired to her own bedsit. I never saw her again, but I feel like she has been with me all these years, almost like we were melded together for a few seconds; as though I felt how she was feeling. I will never forget her, even though

I didn't know her for long. I wish I had known she was terrified and what she was terrified of. I wonder if I could have done anything to save her from her imminent death.

The whole experience feels as if it happened only yesterday. It is as though I can snap my fingers and I am right back there again. I still remember the pain in my back when I hit the wall. It felt like I was a piece of elastic, bouncing back into my standing body. It was like it was happening outside of the physical realm.

I had now had two eerie experiences in this dark, creepy and evil house with the dreadful scent, secret doors and men coming and going at all times. Not one year goes by where I don't think of my supernatural experience with Shirley, or her invitation for tea. Every now and then, a story or podcast will pop up about Fred and Rose West and the memories come back. I never watch or listen to them. I feel as though I already know more than I should.

Chapter Ten

BACK TO SYDNEY AGAIN

Returning to Sydney and old friends went smoothly and life bubbled along as usual. Liz and a few other friends I had made sent handwritten letters or scribbled on blue aerograms. Our lives got busy with life and families over the ensuing years, and the letters became fewer. After a few years, I lost contact with Liz altogether. There were no more letters. The memories didn't disappear, it was just time that slipped by so quickly. We had both moved and we had no way of contacting each other. I reconciled with the idea that my memory of Liz and friends made in Gloucester were long lost.

***

Within a year or so of my return to Sydney, I started dreaming. Just one dream, one terrifyingly real and frightening dream. As I had always been a vivid dreamer, I didn't pay attention to the dream at first. It was always the same dream, it never changed, just the same dream over and over again over the course of a decade or more. It was more of a nightmare and it affected my daily life for days after. The dream was strange and foreboding; always intense and frightening. I had the feeling that this dream was a secret that no-one knows, or as though I was being shown a secret.

In this dream, I am floating high above the ground. I can feel the air around me. Looking down, I see three coffin-shaped mounds in a row. They look old, but there is fresh grass starting to grow up the sides of the mounds. I feel cold and terrified. My eyes dart from the first mound to the second. When I reach the third mound the most horrifying sight awaits. A dainty ankle with a hot-pink stiletto is sticking out of the soil. They are bodies of women! Sometimes I can faintly hear a shovel digging. It sounds as though the ground is wet, and I can hear the shovel rhythmically hitting the ground, sometimes the shattering of concrete. The digging is always in the background; the sound is foreboding and it all seems very real, not like a dream at all. After a while, the digging sounds fade but I am still floating above the mounds. There is an intense feeling that either I have done this or I know they are there. I am terrified because I know they are graves— but I know I haven't buried them. I can't breathe, and all the time I am looking down on them, knowing that they are young women. The hot-pink stiletto makes me feel ill.

I would wake drenched in sweat, the bedsheets saturated. My head would ache, I had no energy and all I could think about was the dream. After slowly waking, I would have to sleep more to gain more energy. It was as though I had been out all night. Sometimes I couldn't even go to work. I thought about the dream for a few days afterwards because it took a while to feel energetic and back to normal.

As I explained in an interview with the TV documentary series *The Extraordinary* in the mid-1990s, I had no reason to have a recurring dream that lasted ten years, where dreadful images of death invaded my sleep. It wasn't a visual dream where I saw horrible things; just a feeling I can't explain.

My first recollection of the dream was one night when my husband and I were renovating our home. He was digging trenches and he said to me, 'Come under the house and have a look', and I said that I didn't want to go under there. I just couldn't. He asked me why, and I told him I'd had a dream the night before in which there were bodies buried underneath the house, or that I'd been buried myself

He just said, 'Don't be stupid' and laughed at me. He was simply perplexed. He was digging up an area to a depth of about six feet, going down to rock. The trenches, the sound of digging, the visions of yawning graves, left me horrified and sickened. There seemed to be no sane reason for me to be afraid to go near the digging.

But every time I went under that house I thought *I hope there isn't anyone buried under there.* It was in the back of my mind all the time, so the dreams were very intense. I think the trenches would have been a trigger, maybe even just the sound of digging, but why? It would take me until 1994 to find out.

The dreams began a decade before the first remains were unearthed at the House of Horrors. I found out that at the time I lived in that house there were seven bodies already underneath the floorboards.

Chapter Eleven

1994 – SHOCK NEWS – 'THE HOUSE OF HORRORS'

My nightmares, including the one about floating above three graves and peering down silently at them, came to an abrupt end when the story hit the media and the cruel murders were discovered. It was 1994 when the news broke. I no longer had to fear these regular, otherworldly dreams. I felt that a connection had been broken. Wherever the nightmares came from, they were now just long-ago dreams of young women's forlorn-looking graves.

I was thirty-five years old and had just had a particularly nasty dream; the worst yet, so frightening and intense. I told only one friend who lived in Tasmania how awful my dream was and how it was affecting my waking life. It must have been particularly intense for me to actually tell somebody, because I kept these dreams to myself for years.

Fred and Rose West's murder spree had just hit the newspapers. The story was everywhere—about 25 Cromwell Street being a house of absolute hell with bodies buried within. The news headlines screamed that nine bodies had been found.

After the story had made the news and the newspapers screeched murder and depravity at the hands of Fred and Rose West, I went into shock. I lived in a bubble for a week or so. I couldn't believe or contemplate such a hideous discovery, and I couldn't find out much as I only had what everyone else in Australia had to go by. I was concerned about Liz, but I had hadn't heard her name mentioned as a victim in any of the media. I was emotionally and mentally shattered, to the core of my being. I couldn't believe or understand any of it. It didn't make sense, and I kept thinking, *how could I not know what had been going on?* I couldn't understand how I could not have known murders and torture had gone one while we lived upstairs and walked the floorboards. Nothing made sense. I needed more clarification, more information about my friends.

It didn't take long for people to start asking questions. I remember my parents, particularly my mother, being relieved that I had survived. She always used to say, 'You were very lucky.' I didn't know much myself and so I couldn't say much about what was happening over there. I just knew that I had stayed there and I considered it my home away from home. I was shocked to my core, anxiously reading anything I could just to try and make sense of it all.

I had the police ringing me asking me if I knew a particular victim. They said her name and asked me how tall she was and did she have a child, and how big her bones were. It was very upsetting to think of friends I hadn't seen for 17 years and all of a sudden you have to try and remember how tall they were and how old they were and how large their bones were.

Most of the articles were the same and equally horrendous. It was difficult being on the other side of the world and not knowing more. Friends and colleagues were shocked and wanted to hear everything I could tell them about my stay there. They were glued to my words about my time in Gloucester all those years ago. Most would remark how lucky I was to survive. I couldn't tell them much about the case because it had only just hit the news, but I could talk about my time over there. I eagerly read anything I could find in the papers and watched the news regularly. I nervously waited to find out more about what was happening over there. I worried about my friends, particularly Liz.

I didn't have to wait long. A few days after the story hit the papers, the British police rang me. My aunt had given them my phone number. The bodies dated back over twenty years and my kindly aunt had advised them that I had stayed there back then and so may know some of the girls. She had also told them that I was the same age as some of the lodgers.

The female police officer spoke kindly and patiently, obviously knowing that I would be shocked and devastated by the happenings. She then told me that some of the bodies had been there for over twenty years, from around the time I was staying there. She asked if I knew any of the lodgers back then. I said only Shirley Robinson. I said that I knew her name and that I had spent time with her. I told her that I saw quite a few girls my own age around the house, but I didn't know their names. I told the officer that I used to see them rushing around, attending to their chores or whatever they were doing, and I never got to know them very well. I then asked her if Liz was a victim, to which the officer replied she was fine and completely safe. I remember heaving a big sigh of relief.

I asked the officer if she could pass my phone number on to Liz, and said it had been fourteen years since I had last seen her. I said that I would love to speak to her and put my mind at ease, and possibly

Chapter Eleven – 1994 – SHOCK NEWS – 'THE HOUSE OF HORRORS'

reunite with her. I didn't know if they would pass on my number and I wasn't expecting them to while they were extremely busy with this new and terrifying case. To my surprise and delight, they were obliging and very understanding and gave my number to Liz. I can never express my gratitude enough. That one gesture was all it took for us to become friends again.

About a week or so after the call from the police, my phone rang. It was Liz. I was surprised and happily taken aback. I wasn't expecting her call. She still had her gentle, soft Gloucester accent. I have always loved that accent and it was a delight to hear it again, even if it was only over the phone. I was tongue-tied at first and didn't know where to start. There was so much to talk about. I felt warm, salty tears run down my cheeks. My heart skipped a beat. My tears were of pure relief that she was safe. We had so much to talk about. We spoke about our families first and filled each other in on our lives.

Liz then told me things I didn't want to hear. She said clearly over the phone, 'Ka, when you were staying here there were seven bodies of young women under the floorboards as we walked out the front door.' Back then, the thought of us walking over the bodies of young and innocent women would have been impossible. My heart sank and I once again felt an abject sickening in the pit of my stomach. I felt like it was in a tight ball of shock. I found it difficult to believe. But it was Liz's gentle voice talking to me and relating what I didn't want to know.

She spoke softly, telling me about Shirley being murdered in her room, with Liz's own belt. Liz said that she was strangled on the very spot where we had been talking. I thought my heart was going to stop. I felt guilty for not being aware of Shirley's fear before her murder. I knew then that Shirley and I were connected in some spiritual or special way. She must have known she was in imminent danger and I felt her energy, and that was the reason I had been flung against the wall—because she was terrified of Fred. I heard that Shirley was buried in the small backyard with other young girls, along with her baby. It was devastating, and difficult to believe any of it.

Liz filled me in on things I could not even imagine could ever occur around me. She told me that Shirley was pregnant with Fred's baby and that that Rose had been jealous of Shirley. Liz was not sure whether Fred or Rose had strangled Shirley, but she was extremely upset by it all. I thought about the book we'd spoken about writing. I thought how everything we gossiped about— and joked that we would write about—was actually true. Our chatter about all the insane things that Rose and Fred were doing was all true. I couldn't believe that all this was going on at the same time we traipsed up the stairs to the top floor.

Liz also told me that Heather, the beautiful little girl that I saw hanging around Rose sometimes, was murdered by Fred in the house. She told me Heather had been strangled and buried beneath the veranda. I had not heard any of these details before, but then again, I didn't see everything. Liz was very fond of Heather and her voice quietened when she whispered about her death at the hands of her father.

On hearing these stories from Liz, shock soaked my very being, almost seeping into my skin. I tried to not get too upset at the things she told me. It all sounded too unbelievable. My skin crawled as I listened to everything that had been kept a secret for decades. It had been going on during the time I had spent there, all those years ago. It was as though I sidestepped a terrible death, but fate didn't have that in mind, not for me. My whole equilibrium felt off balance and I was glad that I was seated while she told me unspeakable things.

Liz then stated sadly, and what seemed nervously, that how since the story had become world news she had had to uproot her family and move. She had four young children, and I thought how daunting it would have been for her and her family to be in the spotlight of a

Chapter Eleven – 1994 – SHOCK NEWS – 'THE HOUSE OF HORRORS'

murder. Even over the phone I could hear how devastated Liz was by all this as she had lived there so long and was fond of Rose, Fred and their children.

She had no idea that while she was lodging upstairs, the degrading and disgusting atrocities were occurring in the darkness of the cellar. I couldn't even contemplate how shocked and horrified she would have been. Four years is a long time to live upstairs in Fred and Rose West's house of horror. I was her guest for one year. My time spent living with her upstairs was a tiny speck of time compared to hers.

The nightmare and shock of what went on while I was there invaded my every thought for weeks on end after our call ended. I analysed every little moment of my time there, looking for clues. I'd had my supernatural experiences, but nothing tangible. The shock of it invaded my life for a period of time, until it settled in. The newspapers and TV channels showed images of the house and it all felt just so shocking and extremely sad. I couldn't stop thinking of Shirley Robinson and all the other innocent young women who lost their lives in that hellish abode.

Liz and I talked often over the next week or so and we decided that I would fly to England and we would catch up. I couldn't wait. My mind would wander back to 1977 and what it was like for us then, in particular our barmaid jobs. It was like a closure of some sort. Even though it was under terrible circumstances, I was excited to see her and counted down the days. After a few weeks, I hadn't heard from Liz, until a letter arrived in the mail. I hastily tore it open. I was wondering why she hadn't called, but I was relieved to hear from her in any way I could. I was expecting the letter to have dates she would like us to meet up over in England.

The only words on the cream paper were scrawled in blue ink, *I'm sorry Ka, I've got cancer.* There was nothing else. I turned the page over, but it was empty. My heart missed a beat. There was no plan to meet up. I quickly found her phone number and rang as speedily as possible. The number rang out; not in service. I sent two or three letters to the only address I had, hoping they would reach her. But I never heard back from her. There wasn't even a 'Return to Sender' letter. Once again, I was shattered. I truly believed with all my heart that we would meet up again. If there was one positive thing in this whole horrific story, it was to reconnect with my friend from decades ago, bringing healing and closure for both of us.

After a week or so, I started to analyse everything. I pondered over the thought that maybe, just maybe, she didn't want to see me again as she wanted to just forget about that period in her life altogether, me included. Maybe she didn't want to associate with me because it would give her too much grief, too much heartache, and she wanted to annihilate the shock of the whole thing. I could understand that entirely. I could understand her running away and obtaining a new identity for herself and her family in a quiet country hamlet or insignificant town. She could have moved to another country just to escape from the shock and horror of it. I think I would have moved away too. I would have run away if I had been living in such a toxic house for so many years. I would want to be away from inquisitive eyes and questions. All I knew in that moment was that I wouldn't get to see my friend again. I was distraught. My heart felt a heaviness once again. I can still see the black words scribbled on the page if I close my eyes. I knew I would never discover anything else that was secretive or that I wasn't aware of at the time, but I didn't care. I didn't want to know any more. It was Liz I grieved for now.

By now Liz was in her early thirties and I thought how cruel it was that she had cancer so young, after surviving Rose and Fred's murderous clutches. I knew that Liz would have had no idea of the terrible things Rose and Fred were doing. I thought of how she would have felt finding out about what they were doing while she slept above. The shock could have given her such stress and it could have affected her health. In the end I sadly accepted the fact that my beautiful friend had succumbed to her cancer. I thought what a shame I hadn't seen her before she became ill. I still feel sad to this day when I stop and think of how fate reels its way.

I am just happy that I could speak to her and know that she had not fallen victim to Fred or Rose. I believe we were both very lucky not to have been dragged into the cellar. From what I have heard it resembled a death chamber, cruelty personified in every depraved way, home to acts that normal human beings did not even think about.

Chapter Twelve

THE END OF THE NIGHTMARES

The nightmares about floating above and peering down silently at three graves, with the pink stiletto on a woman's ankle, ended abruptly. They ceased when the cruel murders were discovered and the story hit the media. I no longer had to fear these regular supernatural dreams. Wherever they came from, they were now just long-ago nightmares of the forlorn-looking graves of young women.

It was 1994 when the story broke. I was in my thirties by then. It had taken years for these dreams to dissipate. I felt a quiet relief that I had kept them to myself, and now they had ended. My mum told me that they were very upset when they heard the news. Mum said it made Cromwell Street look awful; that's what she was worried about. She didn't want people to think badly of the street where they lived. That's how people thought back then.

I'm now in my sixties and it has been forty-eight years since I first crossed paths with Fred and Rose West. It has been thirty-one years since the story broke and their cruelty was brought into the light for the

Chapter Twelve – THE END OF THE NIGHTMARES

world to see. I have reflected on my time there and all the things that went on without my knowledge. As the years went by, I thought about it less and less, but it was just buried beneath the surface.

The story of Fred and Rose West and the House of Horrors has become popular again, with younger people keen to know more about these historical crimes. There have been podcasts and a documentary series on Netflix, with large audiences everywhere of people with a strong interest in true crime stories. This new interest in the case has made me think of my time there all over again, almost forty-eight years ago. I didn't listen to any of the podcasts or watch the series. I still feel that I don't need to know anything else.

A long time ago, somebody told me that Fred had hung himself in prison with his own clothing before his trial, and that Rose was in jail and is in there forever. I also heard that Rose became close friends with Myra Hindley before Myra's death in 2002. Myra was one of the Moors murders duo with Ian Brady. They were serial killers in their own right. When I heard that, I thought to myself that maybe it is true that birds of a feather flock together.

I have not spoken much about this period in my life until just recently People have started to ask me questions again since the events have had renewed publicity. The historical and evil crimes are becoming socially relevant again and people are curious to know what happened in 25 Cromwell Street. It feels good that people are reopening the case and peering in. The young girls who lived in the house, were murdered there and buried beneath the house and in the backyard deserve to be remembered. To me, all these decades later, the house holds torture and mayhem, but also the absolute depth of sadness. I was told the house was pulled down in 1996 and replaced with a walkway. I thought what a wonderful thing to do for the victims of these horrendous acts.

When Liz told me that we had stepped over their bodies whenever we went in and out of the front door, I felt nausea deep within and a tinge of guilt that I had walked over their buried bodies. That is something I don't talk about much. It still makes me cringe to think about it.

I also felt terribly sad for not realising that I should have taken more notice of the strange, supernatural occurrence that I shared with Shirley. I believe it was a warning of something that was going to happen in that room where we stood. I have that guilt to carry around with me too.

I don't feel guilty that they didn't murder me. I think I was just lucky I had people around me who knew what I was doing. I am glad I spent time with my friend Liz in her bedsit, because it was a great time in my life. Regardless of what has been exposed, the months spent in Gloucester will always be an unforgettable adventure. For a young eighteen-year-old girl from Australia, it was just a place that felt like a second home. I had more family members living in Gloucester than I did back in Australia. I used to run around trying to visit everyone as much as I could. The time spent at 25 Cromwell Street will always be like a stain for me, a stain that doesn't go away. A podcast or a news item may appear and the stain gets darker. I think I am the only Australian girl who stayed in this awful house. I feel as though I quietly stepped in and quietly stepped out without anyone harming me.

I will think of those young girls, and especially Shirley, until my last breath. I am taken back to the time I spent in that house whenever I see reports about the House of Horrors. My strange experiences and feelings will stay with me. I still can't bear to hear a podcast or read a book about it. I don't want to know any more than I have been told or feel I need to know. But the interest in this case continues to grow and I will continue to be taken aback. The guilt lingers a tiny bit. *Why not me?* Because I had people who knew where I was, family in the same street, and that is the only reason I survived.

Acknowledgements

This memoir has been a deeply personal, often nerve-wracking and ultimately cathartic exercise for me. It wouldn't have been possible without the support, assistance and expertise of many people.

Firstly, I would like to thank the Hembury Books team for all their work in bringing this book to life. To publisher Jessica Mudditt who assured me with her knowledge and professionalism at every step of the process. To Publishing and Editorial coordinator Sinead Heap for her assistance in the final edits of the manuscript. To Grace Sparkes, for her help in the early renditions of the book. To designer Brad Graham for his exceptional skill in crafting my front cover. And to Alison Hill, whose editorial expertise elevated my work.

A heartfelt thank you to Dane Christie, who has supported me and even brought my story to life in his illustrations.

Finally and most importantly, I want to thank the women, both living and dead, who at any time resided at 25 Cromwell St. Some of us were fortunate enough to escape while others had their lives permanently determined by the acts of Fred and Rose West. I write this as much for you as for me, so that we may all be free of this nightmare.

www.ingramcontent.com/pod-product-compliance
Lightning Source LLC
Chambersburg PA
CBHW020110240426
43661CB00002B/98